ANCIENT CIVILIZATIONS

THE
ROMANS
BUILDERS OF AN EMPIRE

by
KATHERINE REECE

Rourke
Publishing LLC
Vero Beach, Florida 32964

www.rourkepublishing.com

PHOTO CREDITS:
Courtesy Charles Reasoner: pages 7, 29, 31; Courtesy Corel Stock Photos: Cover, title, pages 8, 22, 36, 40; Courtesy www.freestockphotos.com: pages 4, 8, 15, 19, 21, 30, 32, 34, 35, 39, 45; Courtesy Library of Congress, Prints and Photographs Division: pages 4, 6, 16, 17, 20, 22, 23, 28, 33, 37, 38, 43; Courtesy NASA: page 5; Courtesy Rohm Padilla: page 11; Courtesy University of Texas Portrait Gallery: pages 12, 14, 15.

DESIGN AND LAYOUT: ROHM PADILLA
RESEARCH/PAGINATION: LUCY PADILLA

Library of Congress Cataloging-in-Publication Data

Reece, Katherine E., 1955-
    The Romans: builders of an empire / Katherine Reece.
        p. c.m. -- (Ancient Civilizations)
    Includes bibliographical references and index.
    ISBN 1-59515-507-4 (hardcover)

TITLE PAGE IMAGE
Ruins of the Temple of Saturn, Rome

Printed in the USA.

TABLE OF CONTENTS

INTRODUCTION ... 4

Chapter I
WHERE WAS ANCIENT ROME? ... 5

Chapter II
WHO WERE THE ANCIENT ROMANS? ... 7

Chapter III
DAILY LIFE IN THE ROMAN EMPIRE ... 18

Chapter IV
WHAT DID ANCIENT ROMANS EAT? ... 25

Chapter V
WHAT DID ANCIENT ROMANS WEAR? ... 27

Chapter VI
TRADE AND COMMERCE ... 31

Chapter VII
PHILOSOPHY, SCIENCE, ART, AND ARCHITECTURE ... 33

Chapter VIII
BELIEFS AND GODS ... 37

Chapter IX
THE PEOPLE TODAY ... 40

A Timeline of the History of Ancient Rome ... 44

Glossary ... 46

Books of Interest ... 47

Web Sites ... 47

Index ... 48

INTRODUCTION

Do you ever count mile markers along highways on a road trip? Do you, or any of your friends, speak Spanish or Italian? Do you live in a high-rise apartment? Do you know how the water gets to drinking fountains? Have your parents ever served on a jury? How did the months of the year get their names? Do you know why each year has 365 days?

From a small community of shepherds in central Italy grew one of the greatest **empires**, the Roman Empire. In time, the Roman Empire grew so large that it was difficult to manage. Before crumbling in 476 **C.E.**, Rome brought many improvements to the ancient world that are still in use today.

Sculpture of a shepherd boy (left). Modern Rome (above)

CHAPTER I

WHERE WAS ANCIENT ROME?

The Italian **peninsula** juts into the Mediterranean Sea and is centrally located in the region. The **city-state** of Rome started as a village on one of seven hills along the Tiber River in central Italy. As more villages were built, they joined together as one town. The Tiber River provided a route to the sea only 15 miles (24 km) to the west, yet Rome was far enough inland to escape raids by pirates. Steep hills provided a defense against attacks by land from invaders to the north.

Aerial view of the Italian peninsula and the surrounding area

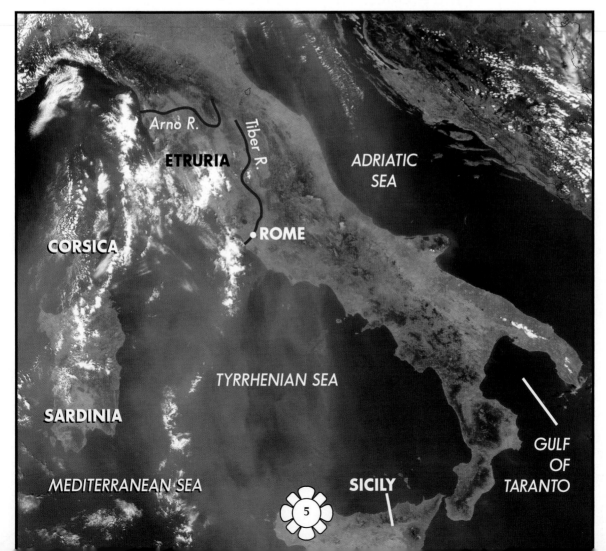

Average temperatures ranged from 45° F (7° C) in the winter to 78° F (26° C) in the summer. Annual rainfall was approximately 38 inches (97 cm). Fertile soils, climate, and an abundance of natural building materials attracted a stream of settlers to the area.

A growing population supplied soldiers needed for expansion as Roman rule spread over lands bordering the Mediterranean Sea. By the 100s C.E., the Roman Empire included lands as far north as the British Isles and as far east as the Persian Gulf. The empire soon covered half of Europe, much of the Middle East, and the north coast of Africa.

At the height of its power, Rome had more than one million people within the city-state and 50 to 70 million people throughout its empire. This is about twice the number of people in the state of California today. A common system of laws and government helped to hold the vast Roman Empire together.

Countryside around Tivoli, Rome

CHAPTER II:
WHO WERE THE ANCIENT ROMANS?

In ancient times the Italian peninsula was inhabited by a variety of peoples, such as Sabines, Umbrians, and Ligurians, who lived north of present-day Rome. The Siculi lived on the island of Sicily, while the Bruttians, Apulians, and Samnites lived on the mainland. Latins lived in ancient Latium near the Tiber River. However, the Etruscans, who were largely influenced by the Greeks, were the most powerful and developed group of people.

The Roman Empire began as a small town at a convenient crossing point on the Tiber River. Latins were attracted by rich farmland and began settling on the Palatine Hill in 1000 B.C.E. Their simple villages of thatched huts gradually united to form Rome in 753 B.C.E.

An Etruscan couple in common dress

ROME IS FOUNDED

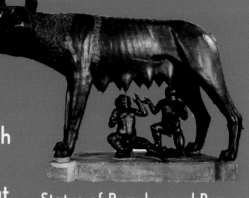

Legend says twin brothers, Romulus and Remus, started Rome on the Palatine Hill, which overlooked the Tiber River. An evil king ordered them killed at birth. A servant took pity on

Statue of Romulus and Remus nursing from a she-wolf

them, put them in a wooden cradle, and floated it down the Tiber River. They were rescued by a she-wolf who nursed them from her own milk. Romulus and Remus grew up, overthrew the wicked king, and founded the city on the hill near where the she-wolf found them.

The Etruscan traders built their towns in the heartland between the Tiber and Arno rivers in a part of Italy known as Etruria, or Tuscany today. By the 700s B.C.E., Latins and Etruscans were the two most important groups of people living on the Italian peninsula.

Ponte Fabricio on the Tiber River

Ruled by kings, Etruscans became the most prominent group in Italy by 600 B.C.E. As a result of their trade with Greece, they learned pottery making, methods of fighting, and adopted brightly colored clothing. Etruscans were skilled craftspeople and engineers. They organized a group of 12 walled city-states with paved streets, brick homes, and public buildings. Etruscan rule expanded to include nearby Rome, and they governed the Romans from 616 to 510 B.C.E.

During the Etruscan **monarchy**, Rome became a wealthy city. Engineers built drainage systems, aqueducts, and huge stone temples. Trade expanded to North Africa, Greece, Anatolia, France, Spain, and the countries along the Black Sea. Rich mineral deposits of copper, tin, and iron from Etruria were traded to the Greeks and Phoenicians.

The Etruscan kings did not have absolute power. Early Romans copied the Greek system of government. There was an **assembly** of common people and a group of elders, called the **senate,** who had some say about who became king and what he did. In 509 B.C.E., the Roman citizens overthrew the Etruscan monarchy and formed a **republic**, which lasted until 27 B.C.E.

In their new republic, the male citizens of Rome elected two men, called **consuls**, to serve for one year. Both consuls had to agree before any law was passed. A senate took over the powers of the king, served for life, and consisted of the heads of a group of 300 wealthy families, aristocrats, and landowners, called **patricians**. Priests, army officers, and civil servants were also a part of this group. Common, working families, called **plebeians**, challenged the power of the patricians and won the right to vote and elect their own assembly. Throughout Roman history, plebeians struggled to take some power from the patricians and to be protected from harmful laws. In time, plebeians elected **tribunes** who spoke for them in the senate and persuaded the republic to have a written code of laws that protected everyone.

Rome's power also grew due to its favorable climate for farming and easy access to deposits of silver, copper, iron, and lead ores to produce tools and weapons. Conquests by Rome's army provided a plentiful supply of slaves. With expansion came a new social class called **equites**, who were wealthy landowners and business people. Citizenship was given to most people of the empire to create loyalty. The republic lasted for 500 years with strong heads of state, a respected senate, and assemblies where common people could be heard.

During the time of the monarchy, Roman rule covered 350 square miles (907 sq km) in Italy. Between 264 and 146 B.C.E., Rome's expanding empire grew to cover 10,000 square miles (25,900 sq km) at home and overseas. Three wars called the **Punic Wars** were fought against Carthage, and ultimately made Rome the master of the Mediterranean Sea. Carthage was founded by Phoenician traders in the 800s B.C.E. and had grown to become a major power in the Central Mediterranean.

A map of the Punic Wars and Hannibal's route through Italy

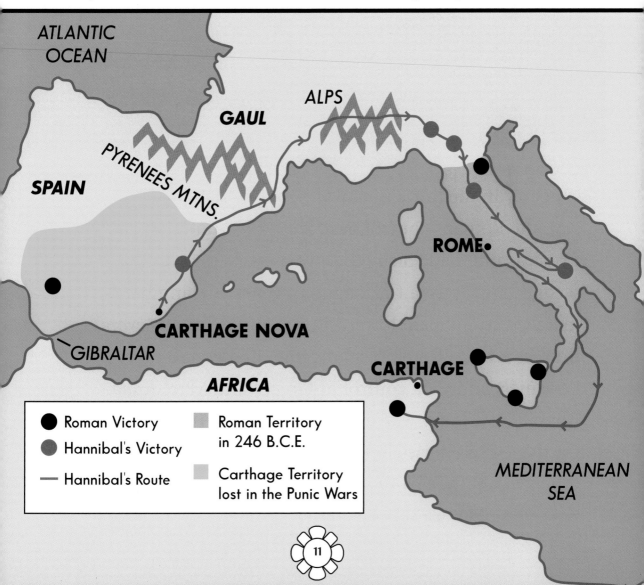

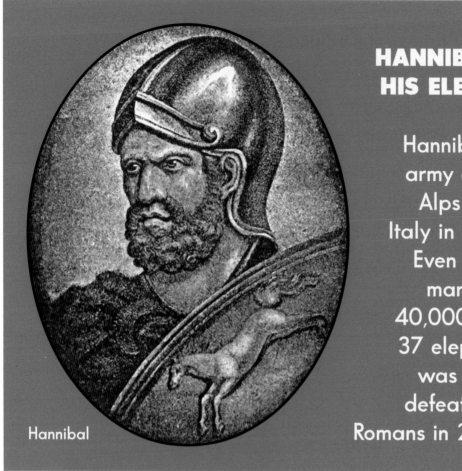

HANNIBAL AND HIS ELEPHANTS

Hannibal led his army across the Alps to invade Italy in 218 B.C.E. Even though he marched with 40,000 men and 37 elephants, he was ultimately defeated by the Romans in 202 B.C.E.

Hannibal

Victory in the first Punic war between 264 and 241 B.C.E. gave the Romans control over the seas around Sardinia and Corsica, and made Sicily their first overseas colony. In the second Punic war, a Carthaginian general, Hannibal, marched from Spain toward Rome and defeated several Roman armies. Roman legions marched east to defeat Phoenicia and took control of Greece and Macedonia. Roman invasion of Carthage and North Africa added all of Carthage's territories to the Roman Empire in the third Punic war between 149 and 146 B.C.E.

As cities were conquered in foreign lands, more men were added to Rome's army. Roman soldiers settled in the lands they conquered, and the Roman way of life spread from Britain to North Africa. Men had to be citizens, landowners, and between the ages of 17 and 46 to serve in the Roman army, and they could only be soldiers for 20 years. Soldiers, called legionaries, were organized into groups, or **legions**, of 3,000 to 6,000 men. Legions were divided into smaller groups of 100 soldiers led by a **centurion**. By 20 B.C.E., the Roman army had more than 300,000 men in its legions.

Common dress of Roman soldiers

A GREAT FIGHTING FORCE

Roman soldiers marched to the walls of enemy forts under a roof of shields held over their heads. They built wooden towers to scale walls and broke through enemy gates with battering rams. Stones were flung from a distance with a **catapult**. This placed them out of range of pots of fire, pitch torches, burning arrows, and stones that were thrown over the walls by the enemy.

As a state without a king, the expanding republic began to break down. Those who were wealthy profited from taxes, goods taken from conquered lands, and slave trade. Small farmers lost their property to large landowners, who used slaves to plant and harvest their crops. These farmers had no way to feed their families, and the gap between the rich and poor widened. Conflicts between leaders and plots to gain control caused problems in Rome for over 100 years.

Roman generals became more powerful as they conquered lands and were viewed as heroes. The Senate feared the ambition of one general, Julius Caesar, and asked him to give up his command.

In 49 B.C.E. Julius Caesar marched his troops to Rome and defeated other generals. By 45 B.C.E. he became the sole ruler of the entire Roman world. Julius Caesar brought peace to the empire, but some feared he planned to make himself king. A group who wanted to revive the republic had him **assassinated** on the Ides (15th) of March in 44 B.C.E. Civil wars followed for the next 20 years.

Julius Caesar

JULIUS CAESAR

Julius Caesar was a great general and a key ruler of the Roman Empire. He was named as ruler of Rome for life in 45 B.C.E, but the very next year he was stabbed to death in the Senate by a group led by Marcus Junius Brutus. His famous last words were, "Et tu, Brute?" (meaning, "you too, Brutus?")

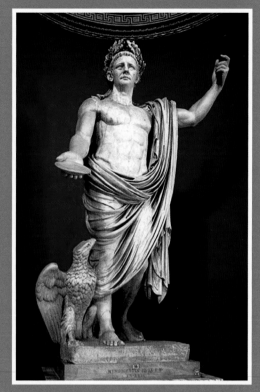

Statue of Julius Caesar

One of Caesar's heirs, Octavian, became the first **emperor** of Rome in 31 B.C.E. and ruled until his death in 14 C.E. Octavian gave himself the title of Augustus, which means "the dignified one." Augustus restored order to Rome's army and revived old customs and laws to rule the empire. A period of stability continued for 200 years.

Illustration of Augustus Caesar

The new Roman Empire gave emperors supreme authority and power. The emperor named the consuls, appointed new senators, headed the army, and directed the making of laws. Citizen assemblies had little power. Having one central head of government helped to unite the various people with their different customs and languages in the conquered territories. People in the territories were loyal to the empire and proud to become Roman citizens, so they could be protected by Roman law.

The large size of the Roman Empire made it difficult to govern. From the time of Emperor Marcus Aurelius in 161 C. E., the Roman Empire had troubles. People were forced to pay high taxes to support the large armies and government. **Christians** were blamed for many of the problems because they did not worship Roman gods. Invaders also threatened the empire's borders. Emperor Aurelius built a large wall around the city of Rome to protect it. Later, Emperor Hadrian built a wall across England to keep out invaders.

Marcus Aurelius

Roman armies began to set up their own leaders as emperors, and civil war broke out. Emperor Diocletian knew one man could no longer govern the entire empire. He divided the Roman Empire into four parts, each with its own capital and ruler, or **tetrarch**. The vast Roman Empire was divided into western and eastern parts. Diocletian outlawed Christian worship in 303 C. E.

Successors to the throne fought for power, and the system of shared rule broke down. Constantine I became the emperor of Rome's eastern provinces in 306 C.E. He moved his capital to Byzantium in 330 C.E. and renamed the city Constantinople. The eastern half of the Roman Empire lasted more than a thousand years as the Byzantine Empire. The Roman Empire split permanently in 396 C.E. when it was invaded by Germanic peoples. The western empire grew weaker and weaker until its fall in 476 C.E.

A Byzantine wall in Constantinople, Turkey

CHAPTER III:

DAILY LIFE IN THE ROMAN EMPIRE

Most Roman citizens lived in the country in huts made of sun-dried bricks. Smoke from cooking fires rose through a hole in the center of the roof. The first peoples were shepherds and farmers and were the backbone of the Roman army. They planted crops in the spring, harvested in the fall, and fought in the army during the summer. As the empire expanded, they spent so much time away from home they had to sell their farms. Common people had very little of their own property and grew food on rented land for their family and for sale.

Wealthy men bought the farmers' lands, grew crops, and raised livestock for profits. The landowners built grand houses, or villas, and servants and slaves worked on their large estates. The hole in the farmer's roof was now an **atrium**, or courtyard, around which there were many small rooms without windows. A shallow trough below the opening was used to catch rainwater. Larger homes had a second courtyard called a peristyle, which served as a garden. Walls were plastered and painted with scenes of the countryside, birds, and flowers. Mosaic floors were set with thousands of colorful stones to make pictures or patterns.

Most people in the cities lived in apartment buildings. Since land was scarce, landlords began building upward. Laws restricted the buildings to no more than six stories, so most of them were only four or

Illustration of a one-room hut in ancient Pompeii

five stories high. The landlords crowded many people into small spaces, and whole families might live in one room. Windows had no glass, but wooden shutters kept out the rain. When the shutters were closed, it was very dark inside, so olive oil lamps were used for light. There was no water upstairs unless tenants carried it up, and families burned charcoal to heat their rooms. Apartment buildings were built with cheap materials, and many collapsed! If the building did not fall down, it might burn to the ground.

Oil lamps were used to burn olive oil.

Roman cities were planned with buildings located in an orderly pattern. There were sewage and water systems, baths, arenas, and theaters. In the center of the city was an open space, or **forum**, surrounded by markets, government buildings, and temples. The wealthy lived in fine houses of brick or stone. Romans built aqueducts to bring fresh water from the hills to the city and canals to carry off waste and drain lakes so land could be farmed.

It is difficult to imagine much work being done in ancient Rome because at one time they had up to 135 holidays a year! Entertainment was provided in big arenas called **amphitheaters**. Slaves were trained as gladiators and fought each other or animals as crowds cheered.

Interior of a Roman amphitheater

The ruins of this aqueduct run alongside modern farmlands.

ROMAN AQUEDUCTS

Aqueducts, gradually sloping downward from nearby hills toward the city, brought more than 300 million gallons (1.135 billion liters) of water to the street fountains, private homes of the wealthy, and bathhouses in Rome. There were more than 300 miles (483 km) of aqueducts, and all but 50 were lead or clay pipes buried underground or covered ground-level channels. Stone coverings protected the water from insects, birds, small animals, and evaporation from the sun. To get the water over gorges and rivers, rows of arches were constructed sometimes two and three levels high. These were connected by a flat bed, and the water flowed in a channel on top.

A modern painting of a chariot race

Chariot races were held in long, oval arenas called circuses. The Circus Maximus held 250,000 people! Romans attended theaters, where they could watch **comedies** or serious **dramas**. Their favorite performances were **mimes**, which were short plays about everyday life.

The Roman Colosseum

Romans built more than 170 lavish public baths from marble and gold. Most of the water brought to Rome was used for bathing rather than drinking. One bathhouse in Rome held 32,000 people! Everyone could use the baths, but women were only allowed to visit before noon. There were steam rooms, indoor pools with warm, hot, or cold water, gyms, exercise grounds, gardens, and sitting areas around the baths. Romans could have massages, read books from the libraries, or relax in the sun.

The baths of Caracalla, Rome

Within Roman families, fathers had total power and control. Children could even be sold into slavery at the father's wishes. A son could not own land or have any say in what his children did until his own father died. As a result, there were many family members in any one household.

Children played with dolls, carts, hobby horses, and board games, but took on the duties of their parents early. They worked in the fields or learned the skills of craftsmen. Children married early, and their parents selected the future bride or groom. Boys 15 to 18 years old married girls as young as 13 or 14.

There were no public schools, and early education came from children copying their parents. Between the ages of 6 and 7 to 10 or 11, children learned reading, writing, and arithmetic at home, or in private schools if they could afford it. Often their teachers were slaves. After age 14, children from wealthy families continued their studies in Latin grammar, literature, math, music, and astronomy. Some studied public speaking, or rhetoric, in hopes of having a career in politics and law.

CHAPTER IV:

WHAT DID ANCIENT ROMANS EAT?

Workers on large country estates supplied a variety of foods. Wheat, rye, barley, vegetables, and fruits were harvested in the valleys. Less fertile hillsides were planted with olive groves and vineyards. Olive oil and wine were stored in half buried pottery jars to keep them cool. Sheep and goats grazed on the estates, and farmers raised pigs, cattle, and poultry.

Food was abundant, but the working man's diet differed from that of the rich. Breakfast was a light meal of cheese and stale bread dipped in wine, but poorer families most likely ate nothing at all before going to work. Families who lived in apartments had no place to cook. The town bakers hired out their ovens, and people paid them to cook their dinners, which consisted of porridge with bread, olives, fruit, or cheese.

Wheat grew readily in the fertile valleys.

Wealthier Romans ate a light midday meal of meat and fish with olives or fruit. Evening meals were often feasts that could last up to 10 hours! Diners would lie on couches set in a U shape around the table. It was common for the guests to bring their own napkins, so they could take home leftovers!

Servants brought shellfish, snails, and vegetables to start the meal. Next came sea fish, small roasted birds, cuts of wild boar, and larger birds such as chickens and ducks, or cranes, parrots, flamingos, and ostriches. For the main meal there was venison, hare, pig, or ham boiled with figs and bay leaves and wrapped in pastry with honey. For dessert the diners ate cakes sweetened with honey or fruit. Trays of apples, pears, olives, and all kinds of fruits covered the tables. Servants poured wine throughout the meal.

ANNONA

By the time of Emperor Augustus, the Roman government fed almost 300,000 poor people. At first, people could buy cheap grain from government stores. Later the government distributed loaves of bread, free oil, pork fat, and even wine to the poor. This free food was called annona, and the program lasted until the government could no longer afford to do so.

CHAPTER V:

WHAT DID ANCIENT ROMANS WEAR?

Romans wore simple clothes made of wool or linen. Every man, woman, and child wore a **tunic**, which hung to the knees or below. A woman's ankle-length tunic, called a stola, was fastened with buttons at the shoulders and arms. Bands of blue, yellow, or gold fringe trimmed the edges of patricians' tunics. A leather thong might be tied around the waist for a belt.

A Roman man wearing a tunic

COLOR OF A ROMAN TUNIC

Men always wore a white tunic. If they ran for public office, their slaves bleached the wool in the sun or whitened the fabric with wet pipe clay. Our word "candidate" comes from the Latin word for "white," or candidus. Patricians had a purple border on their tunics. Women's tunics were colorful, and brides wore yellow or reddish orange.

FULLER

Romans spread their tunics on rocks and pounded them with stones, or they sent their clothes to the laundryman, or fuller. First, the fuller soaked the clothes in urine in brick washtubs. Then he jumped up and down on them with

A woman washing clothes at an ancient Roman fountain

his bare feet before rinsing in another washtub filled with water. The clothes were hung on wooden poles to dry and brushed with **teasels** to fluff the fabric.

Over their tunics patricians wore a large piece of cloth called a **toga**. Once draped around the body, slaves carefully shaped the folds with small pieces of wood and used bits of lead to hold the folds in place. In early Rome all citizens were required to wear togas outside the home. Women wore a robe, or palla, over their tunics. These were made of brightly colored wool and decorated with embroidery. Eventually, wool was replaced by cotton, linen, and silk from India and China.

Footwear of ancient Romans: sandals (left and middle) and boots (right)

Slaves wore a loincloth tied around the waist. Other workers sometimes added short capes. Footwear for soldiers, workmen, or just ordinary citizens was a thick-soled and **hobnailed** boot. People wore thinner soled sandals in the city, but Roman law required them to wear boots with their togas.

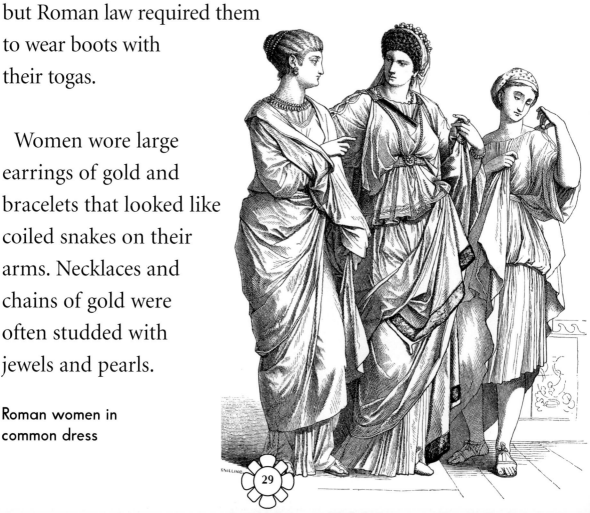

Women wore large earrings of gold and bracelets that looked like coiled snakes on their arms. Necklaces and chains of gold were often studded with jewels and pearls.

Roman women in common dress

29

Women wore lots of makeup. They painted their faces white and smudged red and purple mineral dust on their cheeks and lips. Black shadow made from wood ashes or gold shadow made from **saffron** was brushed on their eyelids. Women polished their fingernails with sheep's fat to make them shiny. Blue paint outlined the veins on their faces, necks, arms, and legs. They bleached freckles on their skin with lemon juice and whitened their teeth by rubbing them with a **pumice** stone.

Women parted their hair in the middle and tied it up on the back of their heads. Slaves coiled and curled women's hair, and the women wore scarves at night to protect their hairdos. Men started out wearing long hair and beards in

A bust of a Roman man with beard

early times, but shaved their faces by the end of the republic. Beards came back in fashion again by the time of Hadrian. Blonde wigs made from the hair of German slaves were also very popular. Some wealthy Romans dusted their hair with silver dust or pure gold to make it lighter in color.

CHAPTER VI:
TRADE AND COMMERCE

Roman cities were the center of trade and commerce. The Roman government made and controlled all currency, but each city was identified with its own coins of gold, silver, or bronze. The use of one standard currency made trade easier between Rome's distant provinces.

Large fleets of sailing ships carried goods across the Mediterranean Sea and to the Danube, Rhine, and Nile rivers. Roman ships had two main masts and a large cargo area. In the cargo area were clay pots, called amphorae, which were filled with grain, wine, oil, and fish sauce. Two large oars were located at the rear of the ship for steering. Carts and wagons traveled over the empire's roads to distant lands.

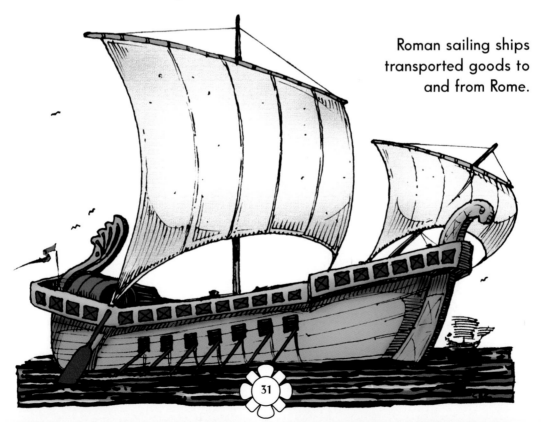

Roman sailing ships transported goods to and from Rome.

Rome imported agricultural products from Gaul, Spain, and northern Africa. Marble came from Greece and northern Italy. Slaves and criminals worked the lead and tin mines in Britain and sent the **ores** to Rome. Silk came from China, ivory from Africa,

Gold coin with the image of Augustus Caesar on the front

and spices and gems from India. From Spain, gold and silver traveled over land and sea. Thousands of wild animals came from Africa to Rome for the gladiator fights.

All provinces traded with Rome. These goods included

Italian pottery, glassware, weapons, tools, and cloth. Bricks, lead pipes, copper, and iron ore helped to build the aqueducts and buildings in Rome.

Illustration of an ancient Roman pot

CHAPTER VII:

PHILOSOPHY, SCIENCE, ART, AND ARCHITECTURE

Rome built thousands of miles of roads, which helped to hold its empire together. Legions could move quickly along the roads to bring order to the empire. Roads also promoted trade and commerce and provided a convenient and efficient route for messages.

A paved Roman street, east of the Jordan River

ALL ROADS LEAD TO ROME

Roman roads covered more than 50,000 miles (80,000 km) throughout the Roman Empire. The roads were better than others of the time because they were straight and smooth. Roads went through tunnels and across bridges, and milestones marked the distance 1,000 paces apart.

NERO'S HOME

Emperor Nero's Golden House was several buildings, not one. His home was surrounded with parklands, farms, forests, and vineyards. Rich and elaborate pavilions were connected by porticos. Greek sculptures were in the gardens. Pipes in the home sprinkled guests with perfume, and rose petals drifted down from ivory ceilings on diners. Cold water ran down stairs and out drains on floors to cool the inside air.

An ancient Roman temple

Romans adopted the Greek style of buildings. Temples were surrounded by columns and connected by a covered walkway, or **portico**. Romans introduced concrete as a strong building material for walls, vaults, and arched roofs. Their arches supported bridges, aqueducts, and roofs so that columns were no longer needed.

Romans borrowed from Greek and Italian traditions for their sculpture and painting. Made from marble, Roman sculptures were very lifelike. Portraits captured the personalities of Roman leaders. Most paintings told of legends, Roman history, and sports events and were on the inside walls of homes or public buildings. Other paintings included peaceful landscapes and still-life pictures of food and elegant tableware.

Marble sculpture of emperor Constantine I (above) and a marble statue of the goddess Minerva (right).

To protect their British province from invasion by barbarians, Emperor Hadrian built a wall to connect forts from the upper Rhine and Danube rivers. This wall stretched all the way from modern Newcastle across the country to Carlisle.

The ruins of Hadrian's Wall in Britain

CHAPTER VIII:

BELIEFS AND GODS

Early Romans believed in **numina**, or invisible spirits that existed in everything. Before any major decision was made, people sought the help of the numina of the night, day, river, home, a hill, forests, or others.

About the time of the Etruscans, Greek gods were accepted and given Roman names. The Romans built temples, shrines, and numerous statues in honor of their gods. Each home had a shrine for its family god or protector.

A stone altar to a Greek god

Neptune-god of the sea

ROMAN GODS AND GODDESSES

Jupiter—supreme god with power over weather

Juno—queen of gods

Ceres—goddess of harvest

Vesta—goddess of hearth fire

Janus—god who stood watch at the door

Diana—goddess of the moon

Aphrodite—goddess of love

Each Roman emperor was worshiped as a god after his death. Temples were built for emperors, and statues were made in their likenesses. Priests were appointed by the government to seek the favor of the many gods and goddesses.

Ruins of the Palace of the Caesars

Around 100 C.E., Romans began to lose interest in the gods and goddesses and were attracted to new religions from the Middle East. One of these was Christianity, which promised happiness after death. Because Christians refused to bow to Roman gods, they were blamed for many troubles of the empire. Romans felt that Christians angered their gods. Many Christians suffered slavery or were sent to the arenas to die. Over time, however, many Romans converted to Christianity, and it became the official religion of the empire in the 300s C.E.

Painted ceiling of a Christian church in Rome

CHAPTER IX:

THE PEOPLE TODAY

Rome is the capital of Italy today and remains a great historic city. Gleaming new buildings stand beside magnificent churches and palaces of the past. In the northwestern corner of Rome is **Vatican** City, the governing and spiritual center of the Roman Catholic Church.

Tourists from all around the world travel to Rome to enjoy the masterpieces of the past and to stroll through the city's fashionable shops. Open-air markets are filled with vendors. Romans and tourists take in the city in horse-drawn carriages or relax at sidewalk cafes. Soccer, basketball, boxing, and tennis are favorite sports.

St. Peter's Basilica, Vatican City, Rome

Rome's 2,775,250 million people live in a city that spreads over 20 hills on both banks of the Tiber River, including the seven famous hills on which ancient Rome was built. The city is

A bank in modern Rome

connected by busy streets lined with banks, hotels, luxury shops, office buildings, restaurants, and theaters. The streets are active with buses, streetcars, taxis, and trolleys. Railroads and highways connect Rome to other cities in Italy. Some of Rome's ancient roads are still in use today.

Most people earn their living through jobs related to commerce and government. They work in restaurants and construction trades. Tourism employs around 20% of Rome's workers. Others work in factories that produce clothing, cloth, and processed foods. Rome is a fashion center and a leader in designing clothing worn in Europe and America. Actors, musicians, painters, sculptors, and writers work in Rome, which is considered one of the film capitals of the world.

Modern and ancient times are side by side in the everyday life of today's Romans.

Education today is very different from the past. Children must attend public schools from ages 6 to 14. After that, students pay fees to attend senior level high school, technical

Interior of the Roman Colosseum

schools, teacher training, or education in the fine arts.

The ancient Roman way of life is present in many modern activities. Our calendar with its months and weeks came to us from the Romans. Laws that guarantee all people will receive equal treatment were first published on bronze tablets by the Romans. Our city planners follow the example of towns that began as army camps with tents set up in squares. Construction of roads, our water systems, the use of concrete and self-supporting arches in buildings came to us from ancient Romans. Because Latin was spoken in the Roman church, schools, and law courts, the language survived the centuries and is the root of Romance languages such as Spanish and Italian. We even owe the idea of numbered seats in a sports arena to ancient Romans! The remains of buildings, statues, and portraits from ancient Roman times remind us of their legacy.

A TIMELINE OF THE
HISTORY OF ROME

753 B.C.E.   Rome is founded.

616-510 B.C.E.   Rome ruled by Etruscan kings.

509 B.C.E.   Romans drive out the Etruscans and set up a republic.

264-241 B.C.E.   First war in Carthage.

218 B.C.E.   Second war in Carthage. Hannibal crosses the Pyrenees.

200 B.C.E.   Rome begins conquest of Mediterranean.

146 B.C.E.   Romans defeat Carthage, Corinth, Macedonia, and Greece, as well as most other countries in the area.

58-51 B.C.E.   Julius Caesar conquers Celts in Gaul.

44 B.C.E.   Julius Caesar is murdered in Rome.

27 B.C.E.   Augustus becomes first Roman emperor until his death in 14 B.C.E.

117-138 C.E.	The emperor Hadrian builds a wall across England.
161-180 C.E.	Marcus Aurelius is emperor.
235 C.E.	Barbarian invasions and civil wars begin.
270-275 C.E.	The emperor Aurelius builds a wall around the city of Rome.
285-305 C.E.	Diocletian is emperor.
330 C.E.	Dedication of city of Constantinople.
395 C.E.	The Roman Empire is split into two parts, east and west.
476 C.E.	The last Roman Emperor of West Roman Empire is overthrown by Germanic tribes.

Ancient stone bakeries in Rome

GLOSSARY

Amphitheater-A round or oval building without a roof that has a central open space surrounded by tiers of seats used by the ancient Romans for public entertainments.

Assassinate-To kill a public leader by a sudden, violent attack.

Assembly-The public meeting of the government of a city where all citizens could take part and vote.

Atrium-The central area in a building, open to the sky.

Catapult- A large wooden beam with a sling hanging from it. Stones were loaded in the sling and flung long distances.

C.E.-A time period beginning with the year of Christ's birth. Also known as Common Era or Christian Era, and abbreviated A.D.

Centurion-In ancient Rome, the leader of 100 soldiers.

Christian-Somebody who believes that Jesus Christ was sent to the world by God to save mankind, and who tries to follow his teachings and example.

City-state-An independent state consisting of the city and surrounding land with its own government, laws, and armies.

Comedy-Story that is acted out and makes us laugh.

Consul-Either of two men, elected to serve for one year as the chief magistrate of the Roman republic.

Drama-Story about a conflict that is acted out.

Emperor-A man who rules an empire.

Empire-A group of countries under one ruler.

Equites-The privileged class of ancient Romans, ranking just below the senators, whose members served as cavalry.

Forum-A public square or market-place in ancient Roman cities where business was conducted and the law courts were situated.

Hobnailed-A heavy boot or shoe that has nails hammered into the bottom to make it last longer.

Legion-In ancient Rome, a large unit of 3,000 to 6,000 soldiers. Those soldiers were called legionaries.

Mime-A play using only body actions and facial expressions and no words.

Monarchy-A political system where a state is ruled by a single person who has power for life and then passes rule to his sons and grandsons.

Numina-A spirit believed to live in an object or control a place (especially in ancient Roman religion).

Ore-A metal-bearing mineral valuable enough to be mined.

Patrician-A member of an aristocratic family of ancient Rome, whose privileges included the exclusive right to hold certain offices.

Peninsula-Land with water on three sides.

Plebeians-One of the common people of ancient Rome.

Portico-A covered walkway leading to a main entrance that consists of a roof supported by pillars.

Pumice-A light glass formed on the top of some lavas and used as an abrasive.

Punic Wars-Three wars between Carthage and Rome that resulted in the destruction of Carthage and its joining to the Roman Empire.

Republic-A form of government whose head is not a king or queen.

Saffron- A plant used for makeup and flavoring foods.

Senate-In ancient Rome, a group of wealthy men who had some power in what the king or emperor did and laws that were passed.

Teasel-A prickly plant with flowers covered with hooked leaves. Romans used the heads to fluff fabric.

Tetrarch-A Roman ruler of a quarter of the country.

Toga-A one-piece cloak worn by men in ancient Rome.

Tribune-A representative of the common people in the ancient Roman republic.

Tunic-A loose-fitting garment of various lengths often tied at the waist.

Vatican-The world's smallest independent nation and headquarters of the Roman Catholic Church.

Books of Interest

Bardi, Piero. *The Atlas of the Classical World.* New York: Peter Bedrick Books, 1997.

Burrell, Roy. *The Romans.* Oxford University Press, 1991.

Carlson, Laurie. *Classical Kids.* Chicago Review Press, 1998.

Harris, Nathaniel. *History of Ancient Rome.* Barnes and Noble Books. 2004.

Martell, Hazel Mary. *The Kingfisher Book of The Ancient World.* New York: Larousse Kingfisher Chambers, Inc., 1995.

Payne, Robert. *Ancient Rome.* New York: ibooks, inc., 2001.

Scarre, Chris. *The Penguin Historical Atlas of Ancient Rome.* Penguin Books Ltd., 1995.

Web Sites

http://members.aol.com/Donnclass/Romelife.html

http://www.bbc.co.uk/schools/romans/

INDEX

Africa 6, 12,13, 32

amphitheaters 20

aqueducts 9, 20, 21, 32, 34

Arno River 8

Augustus Caesar 15, 26

Black Sea 9

British Isles 6

Byzantine Empire 6

Carthage 11, 12

Christianity 39

Circus Maximus 22

Constantine I 17

Constantinople 17

Diocletian 17

Etruria 8, 9

Etruscans 7, 8, 9, 37

Europe 6

forum 20

Greece 9, 12

Hadrian, Emperor 16, 30, 36

Hannibal 12

Italy 11, 12, 41

Julius Caesar 14, 15

Marcus Aurelius 16

Mediterranean Sea 5, 6, 11, 31

Middle East 6, 39

Nero 34

Palatine Hill 7, 8

patricians 10, 27, 28

Persian Gulf 6

Phoenicians 9, 11

plebeians 10

Punic Wars 11, 12

Romulus and Remus 8

Sicily 7, 12

Tiber River 5, 7, 8, 41

Tuscany 8

Vatican City 40

Katherine E. Reece is a native of Georgia, where she grew up in a small town located in the foothills of the Blue Ridge Mountains. She has traveled throughout the United States, Europe, Australia, and New Zealand. Katherine completed her Bachelor of Fine Arts with an emphasis in studio art at the University of Colorado in Boulder, Colorado, where she now resides. Her extensive studies in art history gives her an appreciation for all that can be learned about the culture, beliefs, and traditions of ancient civilizations from the architecture, artifacts, and recordings that have been preserved through the centuries.